Ambulances & Dreamers

Bel Schenk was born and raised in Adelaide and now resides in Melbourne. She is currently the Artistic Director of Express Media, an organisation dedicated to developing and encouraging young writers.

Ambulances & Dreamers

Bel Schenk

Wakefield
Press

Wakefield Press
1 The Parade West
Kent Town
South Australia 5067
www.wakefieldpress.com.au

First published 2008

Cover designed by Liz Nicholson, designBITE
Text designed and typeset by Ryan Paine, Bovine Industries, Melbourne
Printed in Australia by Griffin Digital, Adelaide

National Library of Australia
Cataloguing-in-Publication entry

Author: Schenk, Bel.
Title: Ambulances & dreamers/Bel Schenk.
ISBN: 978 1 86254 818 3 (pbk.).
Dewey Number: A821.4.

For Sonja Dechian

Begin with a Gift

Begin to read
and find an inscription on page 27
proof that you are paying attention
(*I am. Please don't worry. I am.*)
and a kind of test.

Contents

The night is full of ambulances and dreamers.

Peter Bakowski

Solitude. This is Not Lonely.

Evening, and a transport system pressing through the rain.
The timetable folded, a napkin of schedules.
What else can we put on the side of this bus
but suggestions for something to buy?
Perhaps advice or movie screens.

Not from being pounded,
heavy hearts beat slower
from having nowhere to go
but home. I am going home.

The traffic is empty noise from the living room.
Eyes facing the television by habit and design.
I have winter reading and Radox bubbles.
Killing time, like soldiers.

The long evening ends with tea leaves that predict
I will wake running from a black spider
with legs as high as buildings.
At last, something different to fear. Lie still

break the silence with a sigh
and a flush of the toilet
confirming the things that work here.
I would like to float back to sleep
gracefully, like an orchestra looking up
at the ballerina twirling in time.

Birthday Dinner

We sit around wine cups
our accessories catching one another's eyes.
Anecdotes getting wiser.
Partners familiar.

I am looking for something
on the Lazy Susan.
I am looking for someone to spin me the dumplings,
to spin me the light bulb
above the brain
of the comic strip hero.
Please friends, spin me the urge to grow up.

We find
in the embarrassment of the photo album
relief in the present.

But tonight, not to do it all again
not to change it …

someone just spin me the button
to pause it,

there …

the freeze of a movie embrace
the dull ache of a last kiss
the numbness of the still.

To Put Sense into Words

Tonight, in a haze of whisky and beer
you will leave a note for the waitress
under your tip.
You will take her home,
ask her about music.
In the taxi,
brush her breast
as you reach over
to open her door.

She will sing to you
two hours later.
You will say something meaning *thank you*
in the second between awake and sleep
and in your morning half-dream, you will wonder about women –
whether they have ever made sense to you.

Your mother calls
at four in the morning,
forgetting about time differences and, for a moment,
her medication.

Says she wanted to say hello.

You say *your pills are in the bathroom cabinet, Mum.*

She says *of course they are, dear. That makes perfect sense.*

You say *goodbye* and remember how you loved being around her at times of confusion. Times of bullying and crushes.

From a phone booth,
the night before her birthday,
you leave a message on her machine.

Nothing makes sense any more

and play her a song from your headphones
and say *even this*

to the drum beat

even this makes no sense.

What kind of place
do we live in
when we can't make sense of a song?

In the Kitchen, You Cook

Do not confuse your success in
business with happiness
– fortune cookie message

A pink salmon, caught at dawn this morning
lies on the chopping board.
The silent move of your knife
scars the skin and rests on the wood.

Dropped in white wine vinegar,
scallions and ginger make tiny splashes.
Your index finger
steers a whirlpool.

You sweat under
the cuffs and collar of your shirt.
Lemons ripen as you scrape them naked.
Limes, oranges and melons
lie in boxes at your feet.
You kick at them.
It helps you to breathe.

Ken shouts you an order
and you shout back.
This is the game

and you play it well.
You will share some beers on Saturday.

As the ducks hang downside in the window
like school kids on the monkey bars,
you toss and catch the tangled mistake of soggy noodles.
Tonight, it is all wrong.
It does not look right. It will not taste right.
Not tonight.

Begin again
from the top.
Chop quick. Chop quick.

You overhear something:
I can't eat with knitting needles.
It has made you laugh inside.
One time soon you will tell someone about this.

A stocktake of freshness.
You will need:
lychees
squid
won ton wrappers
a taxi home to your rented room
bean sprouts
Chinese cabbage

somebody lovely to cook for …

red peppers

tofu

chickens

somebody to flirt with

at the grocery store …

bok choy and basil

… while waiting in line.

Thoughts about Laundry and You

Trust me.
There are places lonelier than a Sunday night laundromat.
Like a bus station in Middle America.
I am waiting for my clothes.
You are waiting to go somewhere else.
Even with a book, or a beer, the waiting is lonely.
Here, I am washing off weekly smells,
while somewhere in a bus station bathroom,
with those blue heroin lights,
you are gathering them.

Your clothes make a puzzle,
fitting together in your backpack.
Mine spin like chaos, but when viewed closely,
I see patterns of red stripes following beige spots
every three seconds.
The dangerous drop to the bottom,
floating and falling,
like children in rivers,
diving for stones.

The abundance of socks suggests changing weather.

It all comes off in the wash.
On Monday afternoon I stained my jeans with pen,
writing a postcard on my lap. Addressed to you:
The Bus Station

In America
Earth. The Universe.
Infinity.
It all comes off quite simply,
in the hum and the rhythm of the waves.

I am flicking through pretty pages in *Vogue*,
fancying dresses demanding levels of care I will never afford.
I hear the clack of a button on steel.
Did I remove the tissue from my jeans?
Such a delicate thing causes so much damage.
Such a delicate thing comforts so much damage.

Outside this laundromat, people relax by eating or walking.
Outside your station, another bus pulls in.
Most likely, it's not the best, or easiest part of town.
It's the first impression for the lonely stranger.
The romantics choose trains.
The brave choose to stick out their thumbs
on long stretches of highway.
The lonely catch buses.

In time there is a crescendo.
The engine starts and you pull away.
My clothes spin faster.
The driver broadcasts rules.
A girl sits in the seat next to you
and my machine beeps to signal the end.
I open the lid. Start a clean week.

You open a book
and she tells you that she will *not* tell you the end.
You close the book to talk.
Of course I close the lid.
Lids must be closed when not in use.
That is the rule.

Your life is in the pack on the rack above you.
You can see it as your seat reclines
and you settle in for the movie.
I walk home like a hobo with mine.
Wet clothes stuffed and my week gone.
It all comes off. Quite simply.

Silence and Television

Be happy in the world you have created
— fortune cookie message

Somebody has written on the page of a recipe book
17th of December 1977.
The hand of a woman.
Somebody has done this before
with the same fresh ingredients
and a box of linguini.

There are things stuck on this fridge:
an invitation
a shopping list
a magnet from the plumber
pieces of Blu-Tack left from photographs removed.

There are bowls of food on the shelf inside
and on the phone there are messages from
Mum and the gym.
There are neighbours singing upstairs,
CDs in the player – a movie soundtrack
and the best of Elton John,
but cooking is silent tonight – only sizzle and ticks of the timer.

There are borrowed books on the shelf
by whimsical poets and rough travellers.
There are bills on the couch under the remote.

There are programs highlighted in the *TV Guide*.

A text message beeps

I made a salad with those tomatoes we bought. They were fabulous.

You hint back

A salad for one? If not, I am cooking main course.

You wait thirty minutes. You wait an hour
then turn the phone off for silence …

and television.
Silence and television.

Inbox Poem 1

Those lines you write,
I try to read between them
but get caught
in the flash of the pop-up ad
and the ratio of alphabet
to on-screen white.

Drift Back

What can we do but wait
between the hours of three and five am
for the earth, like a satisfied lover, to roll over.
Those little hours that steal doubt
and mould it into a type of fret,
or at the very least, into worry.
What can we do but wait for it
to nail the perfect ten of a somersault.
To see sunrise reappear
like a friend with two full pints
drifting back from the bar.

Daisies and the Chill

There was a woman about 27. That's what the paper said anyway, but to me, she looked older. Something about her eyes. 35, 36 maybe. The eyes always give it away. She told me she was going riding on a red bicycle with a basket on the front, through the forest on the outskirts of town. She wanted to pick mushrooms to sell in the market, and daisies to weave through her hair. It was straw blonde, her hair, with a slight wave and a bit of a frizz. It was the beginning of spring.

They found her body at 5.45 in the morning three days later. The search was called off because of the rain but a few people continued. I stayed at home and slept. No one ever found out who reported her missing, although someone said that a man with an accent made a call from a phone booth, but he didn't leave a name.

She asked me if I wanted to come riding with her, but I said no. I had work to do and an afternoon tea to attend. I asked her why she would ask me as, well, I didn't really know her – you know, kinda weird. She said that she liked the fact that I smiled at her when she walked past on sunny mornings. I asked if we could take a raincheck. She looked at the sky, held out her hand, said *I checked. There's no rain. Come.*

They couldn't move her body because they had watched a popular crime TV show and didn't want to destroy any evidence, so one of the men ran back to town to call the police, who came an hour later. They put her body in a bag. The evidence was apparent. She had died from a head wound after falling on a rock.

She told me that the forest wasn't like the town. That you could swim in the stream and catch tadpoles with your hands. That if you rode far enough you'd see the yokels that live in the hut in the middle. They grow eleven types of vegetables and live by firelight. She said they spoke in French. Or Dutch. Something European.

The paper ran an article. Said she was found with daises in her hair and a broken zucchini by her side. There was a burial. Like a funeral, I guess, but no one really went, so no one really said anything. Which is kinda sad, you know. Sadder than dying.

I said *could we go another time, maybe Sunday*, but I hoped that she would forget and ask someone else. She said Sunday was a great day for forests, especially in the mornings, before people dressed for church. She said she was born on a Sunday in the seventies, in a hospital with drugs and sickness, not in a forest with hippies and daisies and guitars and rain. That would have made much more sense.

She said sometimes you get to see fairies and that wishes come true if they're said when someone's listening. She was like a commercial for perfume with a voice over like: *side by side and hand in hand, we'll run to the river and splash. I'll kiss you on the cheek, like love, and in your ear, whisper secrets.*

On the Saucer

The cup goes around three times
and you are/believe/will do/feel (please circle)
what lies in the pattern:

a cat with three legs trying to walk to the water bowl
a bottle of shiraz
an airplane crashing in the mountains
a boy sniffing petrol
a fast bowler with an elbow injury.

We can choose to live by images.
We can choose to act as disciples.
We can give cheap kudos to the remnants of a hot drink.

You are currently looking for something
that may never emerge/transpire/happen/be there (please circle).

You are currently looking for more
than a cup of tea before bedtime.

The Landing is Harder in Real Time

At midnight
she stands at the top and looks down
at a tiny streetscape,
breathes out again and on three
tumble jumps down.
What does the time we choose to die
say about how we have lived?

Do not pretend that this is sport
(the building has sixty-one floors)
or that she is a superhero.
She cannot stick to windows. Nor can she fly.
Life does not flash before her eyes
leave that to made-for-television specials.
No change of mind
leave that for miracles.
This is quick, the journey is quiet
no reason offered
and the landing is harder in real time.
How peaceful the world might appear
in the seconds before death.

Floor fifty-four.
In her kitchen
a woman contemplates the meal cooked for her lover.
Yet untouched.

I want to win his heart through food
light the gas/sweat onions in olive oil/garlic/capers/parmesan/
    anchovies/olives.

I want his wife to suspect another on his breath
and perfume on his suit.

Small al dente spirals in waves of salted water
and the dishes remain full.

I want the life of somebody else.

Sex and mess.
Lie in sheets, make a joke, watch him dress and
through the window catch a glimpse of:
oh, nothing. Do birds fly at night?

On floor thirty-one
the kids do some drugs.
Many kinds. Not too fussy.
The first timer is taking it well.
Her bikini's off and she's aware of most things. Not all things.
She's in the spa kissing and touching.
Photographs are taken and instantly viewed
and Simon Blake thinks he is hallucinating.
Someone's jumped from the building … Man, don't worry.
I'm seeing shit again.

There is sex.

Sex and mess.

Sex and mess.

On floor twenty-seven

a lecturer writes some notes:

your happiness is in proportion to your tragedy

~~compare and contrast~~.

Are you happier when you've come out of a metaphorical hole?

Meaning, can you really understand happiness if you've never

suffered? ~~Discuss.~~ Show examples. Think of a time when …

5000 words. Discuss.

Call Susan.

Buy food.

Ask how long it will take for forgiveness.

Try not to drink until February 16.

This time, don't hang up. Anything but the hang up. Caller ID.

He writes a note to place on his phone

DON'T HANG UP

Technology vs Paranoia.

… and while falling, still falling

she makes up a song:

falling sixty-one floors

so pretty

I hold my arms to you
and with a mix of touch and luck
I catch you

after the fall
after the fall
after the fall

(A, G and C chords gently strum. Sung whispery. Melancholy.)

On floor six
Claudia changes her light bulb to set up a mood.
Borrows ideas from SoHo nightclubs and movies.
Single jumps to a double-time beat.
We are all beautiful in slow motion.
The landing is softer in slow motion.

On floor five
The fifteen-year-old boy bangs his ceiling
with the handle of a broom
then types into his computer:
Kevin says: wanna come to The Rocky Horror Picture Show
    tomorrow nite?
Donna says: umm, ok. ☺
He clenches his fist to the air –
Yes. Yes.
He looks out from his window:
Kevin says: hey, have you ever seen a body lay splat
by a newspaper stand?

Elsewhere.

Pizza delivery boys press elevator buttons and knock on doors.

Televisions flicker. Refrigerators are opened and closed.

Opened and closed.

Beer is drunk. Food begins to rot and finally, babies rest.

A woman jumps from sixty-one floors.

I catch you
after the fall.

A woman jumps.

The landing is hard.

After midnight.

We might find our life in any landscape,

but moreso here. Each city a turnstile
of details, questions, private moments ...

David O'Meara

City Heat, Walking to the Pub

Cop a load of us
trying to slick down a cowlick on my forehead
that just refuses. Curls up.
We are walking slower than we should,
in the pause of the mix tape,
one bud of music in my ear
while the other waits in yours,
until we reach the song that, in its own little way,
says *stay like this forever.*

You don't need to complain about the weather
when it's all mapped out for you on television.
Dress for it, as I have done,
and treat it as a challenge.
Dare it. Dare it to live up to its promise,
because in time we will be cooler
and we'll want to remember what this feels like.

The Waymouth Street shade has moved to the south side.
Caught us out when we weren't looking.
We walk the concrete, trying to get to the beer garden
and like the snap and whistle of distant fireworks
we are fading,
watching our shadows on the footpath
until the sun hits our pale faces. Cop a load of it.
Dare me. Dare me to handstand in it, hide my face in shade
while the sun zaps my soles in the air.

In the Chinese Grocery Store

You are always learning from others.

Do not lose this ability

— fortune cookie message

The mushrooms have a section to themselves.
We place three types in our basket:
shitake, straw and button. Price reduced.
They are old.

Another old thing: a Chinese woman shuffling up the aisle.
One hand on her walking stick,
the other on a bunch of dirty bok choy.

Watch as she places it in her shoulder bag
and winks at us.
She knows we are giggling.
She knows what we know.

You say, when she leaves, *what a weird thing to steal*
as we look for the cheaper soy.
I say *she must be desperate.*
Do you think so?

Later, when we carry our bags home
we see her standing in line for the streetcar
and she waves.

And in our shared daydream, we ask her to our house
to teach us about mushrooms and greens.
We ask her to cook us dinner – maybe wontons
with garlic and bok choy –
because we know that she cooks
the things that we've only seen
in updated and revised editions
of *Women's Weekly* cookbooks,
or heard about through tales
handed down from mother to child,
and chosen from paper menus with splashes and stains.

Music and Love

Fire up your spirits with music and love
— fortune cookie message

Someone said that we should dance
to the song from my heartbreak.
Let's get lost in sound
and the night.

Let's not think about losing track of time.
When we miss the last train, there will be one
at 6.05 in the morning.
Let's get lost before it arrives.

Someone poured stiff drinks.
One too many, deliberately.
We shoot them down, one by one
line them up on the table, empty glass, cloudy mind.

Let's pick new songs from the karaoke book
and write them down and hand them up
like a pop quiz of music.
Let's play with the sound of laughter.

I didn't know that you were here
until I saw you from the stage
tapping along, smiling at my out of tune-ness.
You still love me, I know.

Let's get out of here.
Come with us. We will take care of you.
I will take you by the hand.
We will get lost again.

To Take Away

You make the perfect flat white
by shooting me a double dose to get me going
as I shiver on the street corner.

Bicycles and dogs pass us.
I count out my change in your hand
and bounce away, after my first gulp.

It will come to me,
a way to say *you make my heart beat faster*
during breaks in television programming,

or when I'm forced from dreams
to rise from sleep
for paper and pen.

Or one day soon I might find that it
hits me when you're
squirting water through ground beans

and stamping the squares
with purple ink
on my loyalty card twice.

Or today when I open my gaze
and dip my newspaper,
the way to say it will slowly rise

like the sound of the applause
for the lead actress in the stage play
as I share with you my headlines.

Val Kilmer is in Your Fortune Cookie

In your gloved hands is a styrofoam cup from which you are
    drinking designer coffee.
You are in the markets, next to the vintage clothes
and the future.

The graffiti on the wall says:

Val Kilmer.

It is the fifth time you have seen *Val Kilmer* graffiti in the city:

On a parking metre on Queen Street
On a stop sign, in black paint, around the corner from your
    building
On a bus, spray painted in red on the mid door, so when opened,
    reads Va   lmer
His face, photocopied and stuck to a wall in the Annex.
Lips painted pink.

A friend of yours, well, not really a friend but someone who
you hang out and play pool with, tells you that Val Kilmer was
written on the wall, next to the urinal at a restaurant, and that
he almost pissed on it when drunk. That he is embarrassed to tell
that story. You promise to keep it top secret.

You compose anagrams:

MARVEL ILK
ALL REV KI
VAR ME KILL

Type his name into Google.

Middle name is Edward

Height is just over six feet

Interesting fact: he never wanted to be in *Top Gun*.
Obligations in contract.

Famous line: *you can be my wingman anytime.*

It is Saturday night and you take a walk to Blockbuster to hire
three movies for an all night Val Kilmer marathon. You invite
your lover to cook popcorn and to massage your feet.

In the middle of *The Doors* you make love. Val Kilmer as Jim
Morrison. Val Kilmer singing 'Light My Fire'. Val Kilmer in
leather pants.

In the morning, you call the city council and leave a message.
You are making a general inquiry about the disproportional
references to Val Kilmer in the downtown area and wonder if
they know anything. If they have, perhaps, funded any projects

to revamp the city. Know of any local artists. Any arrests.
Anything at all.

You leave your number.
Expect a return call.
Never get it.

You compose chords and rhyme lines for a song:

Val, oh my Val Kilmer, why oh why
this is killing me
Val Kilmer

and sing it in the streets. Earn enough money, dropped in your
hat, to buy a morning hangover.

For a photographic essay, you expose images for your slide show
of graffiti in multi colour and head shots in black and white.

You design a spreadsheet. Type in sightings and times and
measurements. You imagine you are on a crime show.
Prime Time.

You stop and rewind.
Pause to fast forward.

Write this poem.
Read it aloud.
Hold your breath.

And signal the time for applause
with the closing of pages.

You look for suspects in the streets.

The obvious: the boy with the deer-hunting cap. The one who
hangs on street corners asking for change to buy cigarettes.

And the unexpected: the old hunchback in the Chinatown
grocery store. Buying fortune cookies and green tea. Laughing
as you …

become obsessed with celebrity.

You design your own fortune. Bake it within sweet biscuit.
Crack it open at midnight:

You will never solve certain mysteries.

This is not how it is supposed to read.

Festival Time in the City[1]

Sneakers squeak[2]
yes, it rains[3]
daylight long vanished; the café bill split[4]
and eyes chill in this taxi ride home.

You squeeze my hand
and I know we're spoiled when I tell you
in a well rehearsed thought
that I'm tired of this.[5]

Faintly heard above the crackles of the driver's dispatch
Suzanne Vega sings[6]
and I think how much easier it would be
if only we were in that diner.

---

1   or, this is a poem called 'footnotes'

2   your sweatshop Nike's

      the ones you wear all weekend

      smell in my bedroom

3   the fact that I am already writing has told you so

4   but you ordered dessert. I didn't.

5   and you know I'm not speaking of the weather

6   *I am sitting in the morning*

      at the diner on the corner

      I am waiting at the counter

      for the man to pour the coffee

            – Tom's Diner

It has been hot today[7]

and the cool change has relieved the noise of grumpy traffic.

As steam rises from the concrete

faces smile and strangers look at each other.

Sigh relief.[8]

---

7   unusually hot. The weather man says to get the washing out before it rains.

   But we are too late. Again.

8   at last

You Like Chinese Food

You like Chinese food

— fortune cookie message

You like Chinese food slurped from tiny porcelain bowls to oily lips. You like it noisy. You like it hot. You like to spill your rice on the plastic table. You like the mess of it all. You like the thrill. You like the accidental spit on your dining partner's jacket. To wipe it off with your napkin. You like to listen to Chinese food crackle. The sizzle of fat on griddle. You like the threat of melting plastic chopsticks and burnt fingers. You like to talk during Chinese food. To talk about stuff that you like: autumn; rain; hats; weekends. You like to watch him listen as you talk through your food. You like how he picks the cashews one by one and places them in your bowl. You wonder if the cashew sacrifice equals love. You like Chinese food washed down with beer and tea. The hot and cold of liquid mixed. The thickness and the thin. The storm. The calm. You like your bean curd fresh and your greens stir-fried. You like your meat to be pulled apart with teeth and hands. Your cuffs dirty with oil. The smell in your washing bag. You like the language of the diners. The passion of foreign anger. You like the quietness of the lovers and the laughter of the group. You like the woman that places her hand to the cheek of a man and a spoonful of soup in his mouth. You imagine them later. You pretend to look behind them at the specials pasted on the wall. You stop yourself from ordering more. You like to stop on the verge of fullness. The elegant sufficiency of a twenty-minute gorge. You like the burp. The taste surprise.

The Pub in Winter

Of course there are drinks and tiny snacks
plonked down on places to lean,
and you are only as clever
as the person you are speaking to.
Placing weight on alternate feet
flattery comes in the queue to the toilet
usually about clothing or hair.
After 3am, delicate people decide to leave with other types
and women air the scent of cigarettes from their dresses.
Mops glide over dampened floors.

For the Details

I walk through tunnels and laneways
running chords from iPod to ears,
creating a movie ending through a song.

Ride the subway carriage,
blink my fringe from my eye,
and join the dots between stops on the map.

For the sound of rain
on concrete and umbrellas
I unplug during the climb to street level.

Wanting to be safely dangerous,
deliberately damp,
I leave my coat undone

and my telephone off
but ready for use
with a swift press of a button.

The emergency light flashes in puddles
and the siren fades into distance
after it passes.

The beat of a nervous heart.
(To love you so much I cry
at the idea of losing you.)

It turns left at the intersection.
Cars swerve and slow
and break the road rules.

Behind me, a foreign language
I try to understand
is spoken by two women.

They are saying a prayer
for the sick or the wounded.
I decide this is the case, at least.

I want the book I am reading
to have the tragic ending
I have imagined

and for the character I am in love with
to exist somewhere
between the subway station and home.

I walk past the new club in town
and the pursed lips
of the girls waiting in line.

Past pizza bars
and beggars with cardboard signs
and the occasional gimmick.

Walking this time of night
is entirely safe.
There are people everywhere.

There are people everywhere.
Walking this time of night
is entirely dangerous.

I turn on my phone to call you,
my lovely you,
and leave one of those messages

I hope you'll save forever.
Not because of the things I say
but because of how I say them.

You will hear accents and music
and the sound of raindrops landing
in the pauses of my speech.

Airplanes land all the time.
Plane-spotters record them on tiny notepads
and video them just in case.

Always have tissues ready in an airport.
For the detail. The hours home.
Then begin to tell me something.

No matter how far you travel,
you can never get away from yourself.

Haruki Murakami

Fuselage

There goes that word again.
So much better than *the main body of a plane.*
Over final call, we discuss what really gets whispered
in the final scene of *Lost in Translation.*
Maybe advice or an address in America.
Regret, most likely. Or nothing. Perhaps nothing.
You reveal that lonely people have changed your life –
the awkwardness of sub-text.

From gate seven, there goes that plane again,
you find yourself on it, and here,
present day, I stay awhile, in this row of seats,
and listen to the beat and style
of the arrival announcements.
An everyday tone in an accent
you are yet to miss.

In the Green Room Café, Toronto

Someone here is reading. Spilling beer foam
on poems. Underlining words
like an undergrad. He is overhearing someone telling stories
about trains in India. Finding higher ground in yoga.
Explaining Zen.

Someone is making a friend from an acquaintance.
He is shouting a round
for someone dying. Test results relayed
from the phone in the stairwell.
Relax. Have a shot of tequila. It's on the house.
Toasting life, there are tips
left on the table. There are tips, given for free
on life remaining and long lost brothers.

For the sloppy service, someone relates a story,
grading the level of importance
the waitress gives
to this muddy coffee. She calls for their order.
We are in a hurry. We don't have time to eat anymore.
No one has time anymore. To eat.

You sit alone,
by candlelight.
Like a poster for a second-hand book store …
writing

and while, in the air,
someone mimes their signature
with an invisible pen

two people in the corner booth
are taking their first steps ...
becoming lovers.

Bars and Concentration Camps

It's a train ride. An inter-city train ride
after concentration camps and hidden music bars
with Balkan beats.
And we are remembering history lessons, Oscar-winning movies
and pint glasses with foam …

and the shots of liquor and cover charges for clubs;
the lines of girls with full bladders of beer.
The way to the shower, the way to the gas,
and the email home with contrasting themes.

In time we recall our guide: *nothing was supposed to waste*
and we stare down the tracks and repeat it on these tracks,
composing our rap, our train ride rap.

We talk …

about the lucky ones
cleaning toilets, chest deep in shit, but far from the guards.
About required reading. The documentaries and tests,
and the shoes and the hair and the skin that they saved.
About the myths, the numbers, the theories, the bones,
the children, the photos, the ribs protruding,
about the women, the rails, the beds for sharing,
the remains …
of the glowing stamp on my hand,
about body odour and music.

We talk …

of the apology
from the German trumpet player
embarrassed for what they did
sorry for the waste.

Nothing was supposed to waste …

and the plans for dinner. The next round of drinks.
About our guide who said he wanted to change the world
and the news I am missing.
Our guide saying nothing has changed
when he reads the paper daily.

And on this train ride. With hangovers and hunger
and packets of crisps, licking salt from the bag,
with plastic cups of coffee and tea …
we talk about writing to change.
About wasting nothing.

World Felafel Tour, 2004

Adelaide
There are lonely planet plans in the sauce of this felafel.
Tahini on your guide book maps
from crushed up salad and deep fried crumbs.
Ideas of eating in each city we mark;
ideas of eating and seeing something garlicky and new.

London
There is jet lag in the bite of your felafel.
We convert the rates for onion on wholemeal wraps
as your mouth moves slower to form a bite.
Slower to kiss and to talk to a stranger,
slower to kiss and to tell me you're scared.

Prague
There are tourists swarming around this felafel.
We improvise the audio commentary of the cathedral.
Imagine stories of death, and kings sexing queens.
We are drenched by the rain.
We are drenched by the sounds of cameras capturing light.

Berlin
You wait at the red and white felafel stall.
I watch you from the coffee house,
sorting out your change, paying Germans with pounds,
laughing with the children,
laughing with the Turks.

Budapest

There are accusations concerning this felafel
before apologies and kisses,
vague notions of wrong. Strange reasons for fights
on the windowsill as we eat. As we eat
on the windowsill to cure sulky cravings.

Krakow

There are suggestions of poetry in this felafel.
You say I could write it
And I think hard for lines, write them on the train,
then discard them in time. Wait for ideas.
Search for my feelings,
then discard them to recycle old into new.

New York

There is too much lettuce in this felafel.
We wait on 23rd for the lights to change
handing it back and forth like a child picking favourites.
Deliberately dropping our fillings on the sidewalk.
Deliberately touching your hand around the bag.

Toronto

There are undertones of love in this felafel
With overtones of chilli. A look sideways as you eat.
Outside, standing away from the bar
we stand, silly drunk on vodka;
we stand outside eating, closing in on home.

Hearts Travel in Boxes and Vehicles

There is no sadness I can't enter
Lorna Crozier

To talk to you on the phone I pause music.
The telephone is cordless. I move around the flat
or lie on my quilt. Some days, I walk through soaked parklands.
Some mornings, I ride on the bus
and speak in whispers and code
to fool the peak-hour passengers.
I know the tones of sadness and distance.
Because you are not here,
I have been kissing the white of my upper arm.

Walking through a dark lane alone makes it all seem dangerous.
My phone rings and I turn my life into a review
of the scenes I'd prefer you to be in.

This town is plump with people ready to leave.
Hearts deep in farewells and thrift store recycling.

Hearts travel in boxes and vehicles.
And when will I run?
And will it be
to or from?

Inbox Poem 2

The tales of your foreign dancing,
sex and sidewalk meals,
gastro and one more postponed flight home,
get quite outdone
by the ease of
You know what? Be careful because I really miss you.

Pauses Between Distance

You call to ask me
the most beautiful thing I have ever heard.

It is late and I have been reading
and thinking of all the things I miss about you:
the suggestive curve of your upper lip
the touch of your cheek to my belly on cloudy Sundays
you singing along streets to a memory of music.

I almost recite you some kind of lyric
but say, instead:
you at this time of the night
as your voice travels through my telephone line.
The pauses between distance.

No one has imagined us.

Adrienne Rich

Notes for Somebody in Berlin

1.

You are worth keeping
like the ticket stub for this museum.
You are worth remembering
like the catastrophe I am trying to understand.

2.

I tell you about my school.
Between the green glow of the exit light
and the echoing sounds of *Oh Tannenbaum, Oh Tannenbaum*
I look for families in the school hall.
A brother gives the middle finger.
A grandfather slumps in sleep
next to a proud father with a comb-over.
Babies cry outside in the swaying arms of mothers.
The chocolates in the snowy advent calendar melt in the heat
and of course the car has overheated.

3.

Back then, Lars writes to me.
Hallo.
My name is Lars. I am 10 years. I live in Hamburg. I play
football. I have a sister. I have brown hair. I like Michael Jackson
Thriller. Your name Schenk is German. You are German?
Good bye
Lars.

Hello Lars,

No, I am not German. My great grandfather was born in
Germany but that was a long time ago. I like Michael Jackson
too. I have two sisters and I am in the middle.

4.

And, the first time I cry for no particular reason.
Frau Haas puts her hand on my shoulder.
Tells me that crying for no particular reason is very womanly.
Girls look over and I grow up.

5.

We take the U-bahn
You take my hand.

6.

Drinking beer. It comes in large glasses.
I tell you that no one in Australia really drinks Fosters
You tell me that no one in Germany really wears lederhosen.
You take me to your apartment.
I take off your clothes (not lederhosen)
in a fog of beer (not Fosters)

7.

We wander streets. Eat lunch inside the bustle of a tiny café.
I want you to translate
Exhaustingly Beautiful

Tell me

so I can describe you in German.

8.

We talk about history. We're supposed to, I think.

I relate the things I know

which is nothing, just text and movies,

compared with you telling me the story of your great uncle.

You've told it before, I can guess:

When I heard about what he did to those people I almost wanted

to kill him. I don't know how to explain it. Have you ever hated

someone you have loved also? He was a guard and not a very good

one. Or an excellent one. He said he obeyed orders.

He said lots of things.

You ask if there are many Jews in Australia.

I mention Melbourne, *which is also a very cool city if you're ever …*

Halt. Stop. This is not the time.

9.

In bed, my head on your stomach, I sing you '99 Luftballons'

because it's the only German song I know

besides 'Pizza und Pommes Frites',

which is not very romantic or classy.

10.

Three days later

There is a 6.15 flight to Frankfurt and I am on it

thinking about the things I left with you:
Deliberately – me in a photograph
trying to look like a film star from the thirties.
Accidentally – my jeans.
Regrettably – my email address.
Should I not freeze you as perfection?

11.

Home and searching
the internet for my family history
I almost want something.
Just how many lives I am prepared to sacrifice for a story
remains unclear
because I shut these thoughts away.

12.

We write emails.
Late at night, I am sharing my bed with technology
and your grandmother dies: *there is no emoticon for this feeling.*
I have an excuse to call you.
You are in the grocery store, buying canned fruit,
shopping in yesterday and you will never catch up.
This sentence keeps repeating: *I feel so alone.*
I tell you to buy fresh and sing a happy song.
Risk this: *the weather is here. Wish you were nice.*
Finally, make you laugh. You say *thank you.*
I will remember this phone call forever.
All the things I suspect about you confirmed.

13.

But, we write emails.

What subtle difference the added word

makes in the same question.

I type *how are you?*

when I should have typed *how are you feeling?*

You say *fine thanks.*

And as the time between reply and reply and reply

gets longer,

I go back to re-read,

freeze you in perfection.

Lessons in Discretion

In the markets we buy
bagels for toasting,
coffee beans for Saturdays,
and strawberries and soy for smoothies.
Finally it is sunny and warm
and the flesh on our upper arms
brush under sleeveless tees.

We admire shoes on girls,
faded jeans on boys
and ripe watermelon discounts.

This afternoon I will taste food
from your breath
and remember the busker
playing Kylie Minogue songs on the accordion
over the spruiker calling two-for-one specials.

I have $2.45 and a screwed up tissue in my skirt pocket.
You have a receipt and a voucher.
We may be stuck in a car park adventure.

You whisper in my ear
something like
you smell so good I want to eat you.
The old man looks on from the fish monger,
and in one eyebrow furrow
gives small lessons in discretion.

Inbox Poem 3

It's difficult to look cool
and to act natural and calm when
the wait between sending
and receiving
is as sharp as the arrow pointed
at the heart of the refresh icon.

At Volts of up to One Billion

How to write this without
referring to the electric current
discharging static through my veins.

It tends to occur more frequently
when you are on my bed, under the window,
looking up at these flashes
through the clouds.

At one billion volts.

I'd like to tell you this:
during a strike, successive portions of air become conductive
as the electrons and positive ions of air molecules
are pulled away from each other and forced
to flow in opposite directions.

Really, I'd like to tell you lots of things
that can't be found with a click on a laptop.

But for now, I'd like to breathe the purple of the evening air
and count the seconds between thunder crashes and light.

Make patterns in the trees
And with every bolt
watch the shape of your face
flash brighter than ideas.

Clearness and Light

That look.
It's there, somewhere.
I have my camera ready and you
sit blank in its way.

Try not to smile
or think about how this will turn out.
Forget about the way you,
with your genes for athletic ability,
contour to fit the frame.

Sit a small while
and look at me, just the way you look at me.
The people we love take the purest portraits.

In time you will see
through the glass on the mantle
clearness and light.
Your soul developed.

Always Open

Curtains drawn and you stayed here
an easy falling into *kiss me, why don't you?*
There was time then. We used it up like road-trip petrol.
There were ruffled sheets and Vegemite toast
crunching over sentences.
Words I'd like to save.
(If we do not talk about such things, did they really happen?)

You simply drove home
and I simply stayed, bathed and
felt relief, like the first cool day after a heat wave.

You told me later
how you admired
the tree-green dress in the boutique window.

I want to say that
if you forget how it looked on the mannequin
simply insert your body
knock at my door and ask me.

The Quiet Storm

We laugh as the weather girl says:
> *the storm is unpredictable to predict*
and about you, these are the words I have used:
> kindness. intimacy. love.
I have no thesaurus. These will suffice.

When things about us conflict, I read the words in your head:
> disappointment. betrayal. fear …

and when you kindly suggest I leave your house,
my natural reaction is to curl in water with a question:
> *am I in over my head?*

Instead I busy myself by washing
dishes and oh, you know, thinking.

All this training my mind to fool you.
Training my mind to fool myself.

Paraphrase

Paraphrase: it's so good to be with you.
You make everything so clear and lovely.

When I was sick you gave me something: food + music = love
and I am not a genius. Some things, I look up,
like anyone else.
Paraphrase: get well *now*. You should really be here. It's not the
same without you.

In my large future, when you enter the party room
look for me first.
My attention is free.

Paraphrase: you + me = I wish we'd met ten years from now.
Paraphrase: person + timing + person = love.
Paraphrase: we'll be fine. I love you. We'll be fine.

I try to paraphrase the look you gave me as I walked the stairs
to your open door:
Legs climbing + twee pop from your lounge room + you with
cardigan and open shoes + closed lipped smile + the embrace of a
girl = things that are all okay.

Seven Different Versions

Your keys unlock the door
you undress
in silence
take my curves
with your hands
lie still
in silence.

When morning comes
you will leave me.

This afternoon I've knelt in my pumpkin patch
dirty denim cuffs folded twice
and noted twenty-three reasons
that you might stay.

A random sample:
we've found meaning in reality television
taken turns to sober drive
looked out to the harbour and touched
and we've discovered
seven different versions
of luscious veggie soup.

Words. Place. A Memory.

You will find a great use for your creative talents
– fortune cookie message

The poem I will write
to make you fall in love with me
will begin with a reference to your skin.

Words (silk. soft. satin.)
Place (your bed. on your sheets. waking from a dream.)
A memory (Barcelona. the window of a train
and your face looking through).

Some rain
and an image of it rolling down your cheeks
like a song.
Think now, of a lyric from a song
for a footnote.
Obscure.

Brushing cheeks.
Lips kissing
and an afternoon
of sun peeping through clouds.

Walking Streets with Broken Lamps ...

and puddles. It's almost morning and we are yet to sleep.
From their bedrooms, locals assume we are drunk teenagers
laughing from our first night on cheap bourbon.

This is our fourth year of knowing one another
and under this broken street lamp we stop to touch;
to say *I want to keep you.*

Happy and awake, this is a love poem for a reason.
In darkness we stop everything important for moments.
Still water reflects nothing without light.

These Fortunes are Currently Available

You will pass the exam by cheating.

Your coffee will be hot and bitter.

People will hurt you.

Time heals all wounds (except some).

Your mum does not know everything.

Sales assistants lie to make you feel better.

You are not the best lover in the world.

You ate too much at dinner. Greed is not good.

The man at the other table is making eyes at you.

He may be ugly but remember how desperate you are.

She is not a mail-order bride.

This flavour is currently unavailable.

You will catch the bus.

You cannot have a relationship through text messages.

You will learn a new language.

Middle Eastern men carry backpacks like everyone else.

Do not disembark from the plane/bus/train.

Your guitar is out of tune. Listen.

Politicians don't tell the whole truth. Some even lie. But some
  are okay.

Vote wisely. Read the paper.

Bad things happen to good people.

You will not win every time.

Some people cannot be influenced.

You are not as ugly as you think.

You are not as intense as you think.

You are not as quirky as you think.

You are not as smart as you think you are.

The person writing these fortunes lives in a tiny apartment in a basement.

There is only one of these messages in existence.

He wears glasses and has white hair.

He is not Chinese.

Look to the atlas to name your baby.

Better still: name your baby 'Atlas'.

Children get teased for having strange names.

If you audition for *Australian Idol*, you will not make it past the first round.

You family indulges your talent.

Your child will fake a cry to get what he wants.

It's time to go.

She lied to you.

Much noise is made when marbles drop on tiled floors.

The saying on your t-shirt directly corresponds to the sentiment in your heart.

Good things happen to bad people.

Some good things go for too long.

You should be able to undertake and complete anything.

End it now.

Acknowledgements

'Val Kilmer is in Your Fortune Cookie'. *Going Down Swinging*, 2006. 'To Put Sense Into Words'. *Artlook Magazine*, 2005. 'Seven Different Versions'. *Interface*, 2005. 'Lessons in Discretion'. Trans. Juan Garrido Salgado. *Arquitrave* 5, Columbia, 2005. Reprinted in *Pendulum* 9, 2005. 'Words. Place. A Memory'. Trans. Juan Garrido Salgado. *Arquitrave* 5, Columbia, 2005. 'You Like Chinese Food'. *FourW* 16, 2005. 'Special Bonus Track'. *Australia Council Youth Website*. www.vibewire.net, 2004. 'In the Greenroom'. *Australia Council Youth Website*. www.vibewire.net, 2004. 'Bars and Concentration Camps'. *Australia Council Youth Website*. www.vibewire.net, 2004. 'Notes for Somebody in Berlin'. *Etchings* 1, 2006. 'Clearness and Light'. *Vitamin Episode 10*, 2006. 'Daisies and the Chill', *Wet Ink*, 2006.

'Bars and Concentration Camps' was Highly Commended in the Gawler Poetry Competition, 2005. 'City Heat, Walking to the Pub' won the Bundy Prize for English Verse, 2006.

Many poems have been performed in pubs, clubs, special events and on the radio.

The re-drafting of this book was supported by ArtsSA.

Special Bonus Track

This is an experimental venture for you. A departure from the safety of previous efforts. A side that may lose some fans but is sure to gain others. You show thumbs up vulnerability with lyrics such as *hello. how are you? I like you* and your five star playful side with track seven *come and touch me* and track three *tie me up gently*. Then something daring and fragile with track four *before my afterglow* and track five *rainfall* in which, under your umbrella, you tell her that you love her, and she turns away and leaves you. You come with stickers and your cover shot is clever with images of pain and we know that you've put in the special bonus track for the real fans, the ones who Google you, the ones who masturbate, and ogle and camp out for you, the ones who follow and post middle of the night revelations, the ones who think the lyric *I saw you cross the street and dropped my everything to meet the side of you that had me broken*, is only for them.

Wakefield Press is an independent publishing and
distribution company based in Adelaide, South Australia.
We love good stories and publish beautiful books.
To see our full range of titles, please visit our website at
www.wakefieldpress.com.au.